THE EMPATH'S SURVIVAL GUIDE

THE EMPATH'S SURVIVAL GUIDE

Navigating Life's Challenges

JUDE HAWTHORNE

QuillQuest Publishers

CONTENTS

CHAPTER 1

Introduction

This book is designed to help you navigate your modern empath life. If you walked into my holistic care practice and opened your heart to me about your challenges feeling different in a world that can feel anything but kind, these are the places you may very well find your answers within each page of this book. Sometimes, I refer to this book as 'a big hug.' I wrote it to feel that way as I guide you in finding home again and give the tips, tools, and time-tested strategies empaths amongst our ancient ancestors have used for millennia to turn their sensitivities into superpowers. Let's prepare you for love, support, emotional solace, inspiration, and the gifts and wisdom of being an empath raging into the 21st century.

As an empath, you have undergone a long initiation and are about to come into a whole new way of life. You feel things differently, perceive the world in a unique way, and endure challenges most people never even have to consider. At this writing, we are undergoing a global crisis in empathy. The natural care, understanding, and kindness of the empath is undervalued in a fast-paced, increasingly narcissistic and materialistic world; and yet it's never been more needed. By developing deeper self-awareness and better boundaries, you will naturally understand the role you have to play in transforming the world and turn your empathy into your most beloved personal superpower.

CHAPTER 2

Understanding Empathy

The term "empath" carries with it a somewhat hedonistic stereotype due to its Carroll-esque coinage and appearances in gift and bookshops. People of heightened empathy range widely in their dispositions and emotional capabilities, with the greatest similarity residing in their pronounced attunements to emotional energies. For some, empathy may be an assaultive stimulus overwhelming the senses. For others, it is the source of a deep sense of connection. In all cases, it involves the porousness of emotional and somatic boundaries that can lead the empath to feel separate and alien from the world around them. Excusing themselves from overstimulating social events or refusing them altogether, the empath lives in tandem with an off-brand life due to their naturally occurring heightened sensitivities. As students, practitioners, and commentators have discussed in relation to us, and we have come to appreciate more in ourselves, a true "empath" is often collectively aware of being unique. For more than a decade, we have hosted a thriving web community of empaths who exchange self-recognition, support, and stories.

The Cambridge Dictionary defines empathy as "the ability to share someone else's feelings or experiences by imagining what it would be like to be in that person's situation." As with any enduring human trait, empathy occurs on a continuum. We all lie somewhere along a spectrum of sensitivity to the feelings of others. Some of us are on the extreme low end of sensitivity, lacking empathy altogether. Some of us have the ability to take another's perspective, but we might need a very clear run-through in order to understand personal and emotional contexts. Others have a natural state of balanced sensitivity to emotional issues, having the ability to be influenced by others without surrendering to manipulation. And some human beings are excessively accommodating and placatory, easily swayed by exaggerated displays of emotion.

Defining Empathy

According to Dr. Judith Orloff, an empath is an expert in her field and a psychiatrist. An empath is physically sensitive and can feel someone else's bodily symptoms or sensations. Not only that, but empaths also have a strong tendency to absorb other people's emotions and energies. Others may describe themselves as sensitive as empaths. You will find a list of questions to determine if you are empathic. Empaths are demonstrably trustworthy, compassionate, and caring about others. What wonderful things to find in your professional self-esteem. Moreover, as a professional empath, you might have asked people to work with or without consulting people in your short-term future. People find comfort in you and your attentiveness since you have this collection of essential qualities.

At the heart of compassion and resilience lies a very special group of people: empaths. Perhaps you are one. I am an empath. An empath is a listener, an open, resilient heart and soul, and someone who has extra-cranking antennae for picking up emotions and thoughts from others. When it comes to well-being and reflection, having someone who gets you and can see through to your true self is one of the best things life can bestow. That is what it can be like to communicate with an empath. How can you know if you are truly an empath? Empaths are highly intuitive, and their bodies respond to their instincts.

Types of Empaths

I approach the conceptualization of "empath" as something like colors—humans may come with the potential to sense every shade, but what actually ends up under their skin varies as much as a painter's primary palette. I'll try to cover as many of these "different shades of empath" as possible. Yet despite categories, many of them will inevitably shade into each other, making it problematic to talk about a "few kinds" in the first place. Some people will resonate more with a breaking-it-down approach; others may prefer to create their own categories in discussion. Here are, then, the primary ideas somewhat commonly identified as relating to being an empath.

While a professional definition of an empath will center on their ability to tune into others' emotional energy within a therapeutic context, popular culture has taken the word in different directions. Empathy is something all humans do to some extent, so one could argue that everyone is endowed with some measure of empathic sensitivity. Given the wide range of understanding, being an "empath" can manifest in many different forms and philosophies. In this subsection, I will only refer to being an empath from the conceptual understanding of someone who feels other people's emotions very strongly, often without any discernible cause. As a community, a legion of books and forums devoted to "empaths" exist, and each has its own unique perspective on the subject.

CHAPTER 3

Challenges Faced by Empaths

It isn't easy to absorb other people's buried pains and hurts, because of the empath's continuous input of energy. It can be hard to recover from these sensations, just as the outer world has harmed them. To the world, some empaths are overpowered and shut down. They may recede from their households and live in isolation because of the overload of feelings, things such as phony diseases, perfectionism, an inability to keep themselves sound, a strong desire to assist others, and a compelling commitment to better a particular predicament. An empath carries these concerns with them and is inherently aware of every single person they meet. Loud noises, odors, and crowds also impact sensory empaths (in which their energies and feelings can be easily impacted). Their empathic electricity can prefer a shallower, more tranquil respiration anytime possible, so they will sense themselves sensitive to breaths. For empaths, a feeling of hunger could be thinking, charming, or mentally distressed. Regular people are often reluctant to eat because they are sensitive to people's power. Suppressed stress could also come when they become pregnant, and empaths can suffer from problems and hot sensations when holding up tense community forces. Emotions are strongly loud or too settled for empaths. When they concentrate on dogs or people's attention during a kid's gathering, they may even watch for many pillows inside their ears to maintain the entire auditory crowd down. Being thought to display or look out of place, such as the notion that an old man or old woman "gets alongside guys," helps make this difficult for teenagers. Empaths upon the power of human empathy find high attack rates. Bashful, scared, and frustrated, when people grove into their sales resource, they can immediately feel worried. Whenever an anxious man goes grappling, the emotional introvert reclaims their energy. For empaths such as relationships or marriages who become digitally connected to the feelings of others, it's important because it is uncontrollable. Empathic males also become important close buddies with women instead of other gentlemen because an empathetic man and woman's recognition of feelings makes them more vulnerable.

One of the biggest challenges empaths face is the feeling of emotional overwhelm. Many empaths absorb other people's emotions or physical symptoms because they are so open and receptive. They can take on other people's battles, conflicts, and life disturbances as if they were their own and suffer through them. If an empath is not aware of this trait, it can be unbearable. Others can accuse them of being cross, high strung, or moody, when an empath just needs solitude and comfort.

Emotional Overwhelm

Let us now dive into some aspects of emotional overwhelm as experienced by empaths. Empaths are individuals who are easily affected by the emotions and energies of others. Empathy can be a useful social skill as it relieves feelings of loneliness, creates a sense of security, and encourages pro-social behavior. Endlessly giving strength to others, on the other hand, entails giving up personal strength. A solid wedding rehearsal, babies entering adulthood, and each change in the life span of empaths can activate intense and almost out-of-control feelings. Decision-making, relationships, workdays, and home life may be adversely affected by emotional stress. Empaths tend to close themselves off and become distant in an effort to avoid unwanted emotions. Empaths may either enter uncomfortable conditions, accept behaviors they do not like, or feel like they need to rescue the feelings of others.

Being emotionally overwhelmed is an unwelcome part of life for many empaths. Everyday experiences, from shopping in a crowded store to scrolling through a social media feed to joining a lively office meeting, can feel overwhelming. For empaths, quiet time alone can be extremely restorative for the mind, body, and emotions. An overly stimulated nervous system sets the body and mind on high alert, possibly exhausting an empath and producing physical and emotional distress. The impact of empaths being emotional sponges can be significant. Empaths may develop a range of sensitivity-related issues such as anxiety, addictions, high stress, depression, and post-traumatic stress disorder.

Boundary Setting

Many empaths fall into the trap of using other people's opinions as a metric as to how they should think and act, which is deeply insufficient. This practice is maladaptive for the empath and sets them up for an emotional roller coaster. Pay attention to situations that have, in the past, most commonly spun you out, such as conflict with a family member or navigating interpersonal dynamics at work, and develop a plan of action to prevent things from getting worse. What matters is how you feel about your choices. If being kind to an abusive friend and visiting them in the hospital when they are sick is something in which you believe, go for it. True world changers work within themselves to change the world. Set a boundary—advocate for yourself to others. Maintain your healthy stress-reducing activity. Mitigate as many contributing stressors as possible.

One of the most common complaints I hear from heart patients in my private practice is "I am so sensitive and open, and people take advantage of me." Boundary setting is a crucial aspect of maintaining your center as an empath and is equally important for your emotional and physical wellbeing. We tend to define ourselves according to the opinions of others, to confuse our beliefs with the beliefs of others, and sometimes to go so far as to allow others to place opinions in our minds. Boundary setting is not something we usually talk about openly, yet it is so crucial for our emotional health.

CHAPTER 4

Coping Strategies

Living as an empath in today's world can be overwhelming. So much is unfolding on the global stage, and every day you're encountering people who are suffering, people you care about, and people who need your help. Here are some suggestions for coping strategies for empaths. First and foremost, always engage in self-care. Your intuition is an important guidance system. Practice self-inquiry to better understand your strengths, fears, shared unconscious beliefs, personal triggers, and vulnerabilities. In daily life, urge to run through these five self-care commands, stopping wherever an inner "yes" says, "Really need this now!"

1. Embody your physical well-being: - Move your body regularly and engage in joyful exercise. - Eat a nutritionally balanced meal, breaking bread with people you care about. - Maintain an orderly environment that automatically sets the stage for a healthy body.

2. Embrace your emotional well-being: - Have a good laugh when you can. - Enjoy some good news on television, for a

change. - Indulge yourself with a cherished treat or a movie you've been yearning to see.

3. Empower your mental well-being: - Seek mental stimulation and enjoy learning. - Create an organized plan to accomplish your tasks. - Cultivate your creative talents. - Experience the benefits of being in nature. Connect with plants and animals.
4. Energize your spiritual well-being: - Utilize spiritual practices that interface with your body, such as reiki, chi gong, breathwork, or yoga. - Establish a meaningful ritual, such as lighting a candle and saying grace before enjoying a meal with friends.

Self-Care Techniques

Embrace neurofeedback: Neurofeedback trains the brain to stay present no matter what external circumstances are taking place in the environment. A person is hooked up to electrodes and shown videos of beautiful scenes in nature, which move and change. Because the person's brainwaves change with the excitement of nature, they have immediate feedback. From the computer screen, they see their brain waves moving in different colors in the background, signaling that the brain is finding a healthy way to respond to the scene. Neurofeedback trains the brain not to get hijacked by the fear and hopelessness that empaths so often feel. Neurofeedback takes thirty to fifty sessions to show results, and costs fifteen to twenty thousand dollars – which, if you can afford it, is life-changing.

Allow time to recuperate: Make a list of hobbies that you love and engage in them, even if you have only fifteen minutes. If you paint, enjoy the sensual, luxurious and restorative feeling of holding the brush and smell of the paint as you stroke the canvas. It's vital to get out of your to-do lists and daily schedule, to refuel and rejuvenate, even for twenty minutes a day.

Take a bath: Hydrating tissues is the first secret to mood management. Fill your tub with water, infuse it with ten drops of tea tree, geranium or lavender (great for calming and soothing nerves), and a cup of baking soda (which neutralizes and rids of toxins).

Be in nature: Being in nature uplevels every cell in your body. It's essential for empaths to spend time in nature several days a week.

Energy Management

Health and Healing of the Physical Body Any form of treatment should be taken as a whole, considering more than is dealt with by the average physician who treats manifest diseases and is not capable of curing one of them. A certain division of wordings will be indulged in where necessary. The colorful malformation of the aura that manifests in our physical system, and thus on our physical body, is called some form of physical disease. This touches upon the physical and mental sheath (which is closer to the physical: nature), their relationship to the soul and Spirit. No method that omits any portion of the entire manifestation can be treated as a cure; the physician—or healing doctor—cannot cure until he knows the latent disease and removes it. The sparks provide for the fire. We provide what there is to provide where we stand, and circle instead of being stuck in, unaware.

Personal Energy You are energy. You have a physical body that expresses your spiritual energy and that is contained in an energy body. Within and around your energy body is the envelope of life force energy. Every second we are charged with life force energy. For an empath, the higher energies of the Universe are drawn to the personality that is the most sensitive and has a good sense of harmony and balance. They flow out from such a personality. The influx of this energy is different to the energies that are attracted to the mental sheath and the emotional sheath. The physical body is a sponge on top of the energy bodies. Our energies are created from two sources: rising from the earth and coming from the sun. That is why people have a joie de vie (becoming one with nature) during that season and they appear fresh and young. They prefer to move in low territories over the higher regions. They do not need the vital, spiritual energy of the sun, which an advanced worker takes in at this crucial period every summer.

CHAPTER 5

Navigating Relationships

In making friends, empaths too have a more difficult time than non-empaths. Not every extending hand is trustworthy, empath or not. "I would warn anyone about becoming a so-called friend too quickly unless the situation and timing is right," one empath we spoke to said. "I have been betrayed so much that it is nearly impossible for me to relax into trust." These empath-over-empath friendships, however, have a special kind of nurturing and support all their own. "It's hard for empaths to create friends because we're so sensitive," Utah-based psychic therapist Elyse Curtis says. Nonetheless, with some self-awareness, work, and the cautious openness that is a hallmark of empaths just as much as that vulnerability, empaths can build deep friendships with one another.

One of the biggest challenges for an empath is often navigating personal connections with non-empaths, especially the challenge of communicating a non-empath's perspective to one's partner or friends. Rosenberg suggests that working on yourself and developing healthy boundaries - as well as learning the same about your partner - is in order. "Realize that empathy, attending to the feelings of others and expressing our own feelings, can have a tremendous beneficial effect in our relationships."

Empath-Non-Empath Dynamics

Sometimes empaths might mistakenly assume that everyone is very much in tune with what's going on around them, and then can feel lost when others can't determine what's wrong. Empaths, sweet and compassionate beings, get so accustomed to organizing their lives around what everyone else is thinking and feeling that there's a level of irritation when others don't make the same daily effort. The non-empathic partner might ask, "How can you forget that she's upset with what happened?" Meanwhile, their empathic partner feels frustrated that the non-empath hasn't checked in with their coworker. There are several dynamics and factors at work in each of these situations, and countless more just like them. For the relationship to work how each partner wants it to, it requires a great deal of conversation, time, and respect for different frequencies of empathy.

For the most part, interactions between empaths and non-empaths don't elicit conflict. Being an empath doesn't make someone superior, and most are happy for others to do whatever they feel comfortable doing. But when empaths feel the pressure to shut down their natural responses in order to interact with a non-empath, they might begin to feel as if their non-empath friends and family members are "less than." "Why don't you just know that?" they say, trying to suppress irritation. The non-empath can see that they're upset, and both partners might begin thinking that the other isn't respecting them. Once the iceberg is broken apart, even a small wave can begin to create more and more waves until the water is churning for one or both partners in a conversation. It is important to note at this time that you often do not have full control over your empathic abilities and that you might burst into tears or guffaws and be unable to suppress them. Many non-empaths do not trust their own feelings and will perceive you as manipulative or terrible. This is why sharing your emotional range with others can be so problematic for empaths.

Supportive Friendships

1. When sharing problems or personal details, confide in empathic friends instead of acquaintances or work colleagues. In the long run, your fears are more likely to be kept under wraps. 2. Because bystanders, including those in immediate families, are often the attackers in societal sabotage, it's important to understand the stereotype: "The apple doesn't fall far from the tree." 3. Start thinking about where you might come to find new people to meet. Reading groups, a meetup group, a volunteer opportunity, a gentle yoga class, or a hike could all be possibilities. If you don't believe in what you'll be seeing over time, try something different. 4. Remember that no one else will guarantee happiness in your life. You're the one who determines whether or not anyone satisfies your needs. 5. Prioritize people who show respect for others, work and are sustainably kind to animals, and are financially and emotionally responsible. A person who is kind and attentive can eventually display their unpleasant or authentically nasty face once you express your desires or demands. Then keep an eye on them.

Tips on Nurturing Empathic Friendships and Releasing Toxic Friends:

Empaths often tell me how much they crave close, meaningful friendships. One of the first questions I ask in my workshops is, "How many of you have one or more close friends who really get who you are and are also an empath?" Only a few hands go up. Over time, through hard-won experience, I have learned tips on how to maintain friendships and keep toxic people at bay. In recent years, the importance of friends for well-being has gained institutional support. Strengthening your existing close friendships or cultivating new friendships can greatly enhance your resilience and contribute to your happiness. The affection shared in your friendships can help reduce the intensity of worry, despair, grief, and loneliness, as well as delay memory loss. If you are isolated or feel lonely, you may have a greater risk of heart disease, stroke, and cancer.

CHAPTER 6

Workplace Dynamics

When the Drama Continues: A friend who runs a program for at-risk teens became the target of one boy's anger for many years. In a positive way, she lowered her energy and made herself invisible to him. This is an unusual strategy, but it may work to direct a person's anger away from you. Navigating workplace dynamics can be complex for an empath. It requires much energy, empathy, patience, and taking oneself to task. In the meantime, pay attention to the quirky ways your empathy can offer solutions no one else sees. Although empathy may not be valued in the workplace, organizations are now waking up to just how much dissing employees - who may be customers - and impeding their external brand can cut into profits through lack of customer service, high turnover, and increased health-care costs.

Lipsky and Berthiaume offer some strategies for the empath in the world of work. It may seem trite or obvious, but the best approach to tough supervisors is what Silicon Valley calls "managing up." Find out what your supervisor wants and what will derail him or her. The second approach to office politics is to look for the silver lining and try to find some good in the difficult person. In other words, don't make office life an all-or-none question.

One empathic CEO stated, "Empathy is compassionate, not soft. I am in the energy business and the service business. The only way to win in this business is to deal with employees and customers empathetically." To be a good leader, it's helpful to have a level of empathy because you need to understand what motivates others to be their best. Good managers address both the form and the content of team decisions. They recognize that empathy and understanding are as central to business as brainstorming and spreadsheets.

Empathic Leadership

The classic empathetic leader is one who pairs enthusiasm with courage, follows a positive ethical path, and seeks and honors values. Yet there have been only a few published studies about 'empathy' and 'leadership', although there is certainly interest in the area, the emphasis has been on teaching leadership as it is being practiced in the corporate world. True leaders, empathic leaders, are also offering probity and resisting the distractions of influence. They're only focused and have us walk in the same manner. Troubling such an approach requires the capacity to see and feel on a profoundly personal level. Empathic leaders don't shy away from the challenges, they genuinely care for their team and the people that they are leading. A fundamental lack of empathy can result in different forms of leadership.

Empaths can make good leaders because they care about the wellbeing of individuals and groups. They are also often astute observers, picking up nonverbal cues and subtleties in tone. "Leaders of tomorrow will need to navigate intense emotionality and disruption," according to the Center for Creative Leadership. An empathic leader can inspire without overly relying on criticism and punishment, instead choosing compassionate understanding and affirmation. The following are primary empathic leadership competencies identified by the Center for Creative Leadership and other experts: - Caring about the people within the organization. - Listening and communicating effectively. - Establishing connections in the workplace. - Conflict facilitation and resolution. - Being open to diverse workers in the organization.

Dealing with Office Politics

Office politics are difficult for any empath to navigate simply because it is difficult to separate the emotions and authenticity of the situation from the need to be diplomatic and "play the game" to move up in the workplace. Continuously feeling like you are manipulating others can very quickly make one feel like you are manipulative, even when it is circumstance rather than your own doing. As an empath, you know how important it is to be genuine and authentic in all interactions. Trying to play games with others is an energy and spirit-sucking business. One way to handle it is to maintain that level of decency and respect in interactions with people, but maintaining emotional distance in those interactions. Keep them professional, ask polite questions about family when it's appropriate and talk about common interests in positive contexts. Try to leave it at that and keep a physical distance from people who come to you solely to send out negative vibes. The Five Marks blogs has some really good tips on how to handle office politics, too. They're done with the people, but the advice is still useful. Go to for more.

I've experienced similar struggles trying to be more diplomatic or not getting too excited about work at times, and it's a sticky issue for I-type managers, too (you might ask a few of them how they handle it). A lot of it is learning to fake it, but because I reserve that for special occasions, my body goes into a battle with itself and I'm exhausted afterward. I've found other ways to handle it, but it's been trial and error.

CHAPTER 7

Parenting as an Empath

The challenge for empaths is how to raise emotionally healthy children when so many negative influences surround them. The goal is to provide tools and strategies to help children avoid feeling overwhelmed by the many challenges and pressures they face from within and without. Empathy should be at the heart of parenting, but in a healthy form—an empathy that joins with empowering. To do so, there are four important elements to keep in mind as you parent a highly sensitive or empathic child. First, you must make them feel safe. An empathic child is frightened easily because she feels and knows more than other children. Second, you need to help her integrate all she is absorbing. That means listening, validating their feelings, and helping them process their experiences by talking about them. Third, it is crucial to set high expectations while demonstrating behaviors. Fourth, you need to recognize and honor their spiritual gifts and nurture those side by side with teaching coping skills. It is a blend of these factors that ultimately creates the emotionally healthy, happy, and responsible empathic adult.

For empaths, parenting is a lifelong balancing act of being present and attuned to your children while maintaining healthy boundaries.

Empaths have an intuitive sense that their child is upset before the child utters a word. As an empath, you most likely pick up on all their emotions: their fears when they have a bad dream, their anxiety as they head off to school, their excitement and joy when good things happen. And occasionally their anger. You suffer more when they suffer, and you are happiest when they are happy.

Balancing Empathy and Boundaries

Here are strategies for parenting the empathic child: Remain as centered as possible. A new theory of parenting is emerging out of many years of child research and being lived in my own family. This theory claims that the most important work you will ever do in raising your children is the work you do on yourself. If you wish to raise a responsible empathic child, you must become responsibly empathic yourself, because your child will be learning about empathy from you no matter what you say, only from what you do. Empathy "education" starts at home with the parents, beginning to change their attitudes, habits, beliefs, and values. One of the most difficult and important tasks in learning to trust and develop one's intuition is to develop fine inner discriminations. As I participate in change, impelled by inner visions and goals, I must learn when to be trusting to the wisdom of others and when to be responsible to myself.

While the parenting field is vast, few books address the unique challenges of living with a supremely sensitive child. An empathic child with delicate physical senses may be exhausted after less than an hour shopping with us or munching popcorn in a loud theater. Triggered by gangs or bomb scares, vivid movie images, and the news that we grown-ups may be forming our Cold War attitudes with children's exposure to our words, my sensory children would chew on formula the whole next day. I believe that we parents are the major cause of our children's increasingly larger proportion of learning disabilities. Our modern lifestyles, stemming from learned insensitivities and impulse-driven behaviors, have resulted in "dis-integrating" effects on our offspring.

CHAPTER 8

Spiritual Growth and Empathy

There are important parts of the toolkit in the spirituality of empathy, or the evolution of empathy. In the early days of the HSP movement, back in the 80s, there was this one very popular form of meditation. I even went to some workshops on it and really appreciated it. But as HSPs, it can go way, way too far. The goal was to empty the mind of everything, a sort of drastic step that can be a relief or a satisfaction to do once in a while. But it is not a useful practice for people whose bodies are extreme. The more extreme your trait, the less it will work for you. The best kind of meditation for empaths is one that is more balanced inside and is more aware of the body, of emotions, and that makes some room but is not focused exclusively on emptiness. Feeding yourself with spiritual influences can help you sharpen your awareness and your intelligence, connect with others, strengthen your courage, and free your emotions.

This is the area where empathy develops its association with the spiritual dimension because, again, whether you're a meditator or not, spiritual growth, emotional growth, and evolution all go hand in hand. In my programs that are about training sensitive people, in my empath groups that I've led for decades, I'm always capitalizing on this idea of working with your body, working with your emotions, and knowing that it has a spiritual context.

Meditation and Mindfulness Practices

Empaths are also deeply spiritual people who seek a deeper understanding of life—both the blessings and the challenges. Toward this end, I encourage you to include a short prayerful meditation in naming your top 10 blessings. This prayer differs from a more traditional and intercessory type of prayer in that there is no asking involved. In fact, the only intention is that you feel your thankfulness. Quiet your mind and take a few deep breaths, and then dwell on one thing for which you are grateful. As you put your attention on it, the feeling of thankfulness may expand into your heart and body. This enables you to feel that internal truth of "thank you," a wonderful prayer in itself. After a while, keep quietly holding the sensation while moving to the next item on your gratitude list. Keep going until you have named about 10 things for which you have heartfelt appreciation.

If you desire to develop your spiritual self—as many empaths do—it is important to incorporate some form of meditation into your life. Spending even just ten minutes a day quietly listening to your inner compass can help you navigate through the daily ups and downs of being an empath. See the first chapter to learn about the many forms of meditation. I also recommend that you include a simple mindfulness practice into your everyday routine. To do this, simply pay full attention to the current moment. When you are washing dishes, for example, feel the sensation of the water running over your hands and the texture of the dishes. Giving full attention to the feeling of the present moment helps to calm your busy mind. Eventually, you can learn to incorporate your breath into these moments. More specifically, simply put your attention on your breath several times a day. This helps to quiet your overactive mind.

Conclusion

It is important to respect and embrace our empathy rather than have it rammed away when project deadlines are missed, our integrity gets questioned – and when disaster strikes at home, we have to play caretaker of a sad family who rely on us every single day to ensure they don't lose their home. It is also more challenging to do so as mum's energy starts to drain more and more as cancer eats away at her chest. Fee was worried about coming back to The School of Life office on Tuesday after finally having that conversation because she feared she'd be pegged as the emotionally soaking-wet. As a matter of fact, she thought that most of her office would feel the same. She was pleasantly surprised to find out that she was not the only person in her workplace dealing with running of the eyes and wet tissues. As expected, she received kind words of love, comfort and encouragement from people who understood that the last month of her time at home had been hard. She cried while she was surrounded by friends who sent words of comfort, understanding and hope. To be empathetic is to live; to be both empathetic and introspective is to be alive.

Many empaths are surrounded by friends or family who still see them as emotionally fragile. That notion can be tough to watch over time. Remember to give yourself a break when watching yourself slip into the old role or even fall very short of peer expectations. It took courage and willingness to evolve the old pattern to be open to embrace your sensitivity now. The most important thing is that you love and respect your life now — not some ideal idea of what you want it to be like. The glory lies in being empathetic even in the most difficult conditions. And the most glorious of the most tragic moments is just here.

www.ingramcontent.com/pod-product-compliance
Lightning Source LLC
Chambersburg PA
CBHW021406160726
47994CB00007B/3104